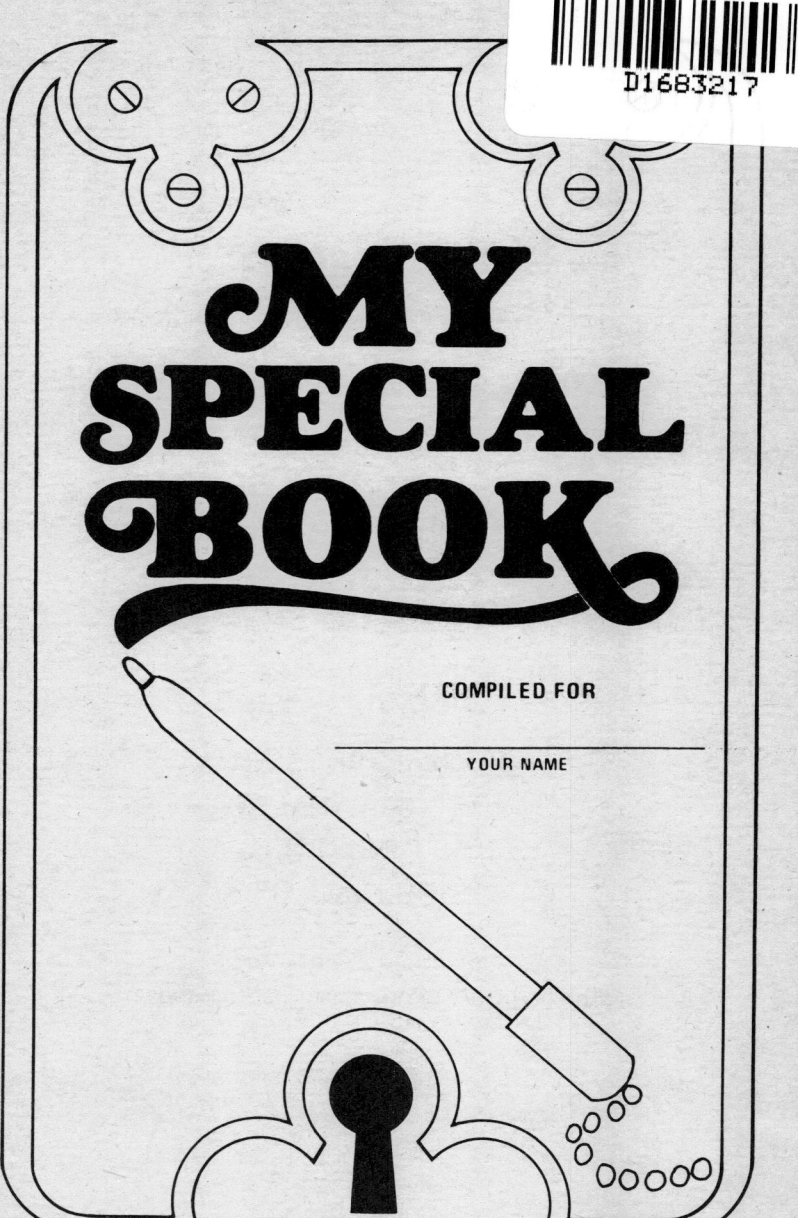

MY SPECIAL BOOK

COMPILED FOR

____
YOUR NAME

BY DINA ANASTASIO

PRICE/STERN/SLOAN
Publishers, Inc., Los Angeles
1981

Other Price/Stern/Sloan publications
by Dina Anastasio:

MY OWN BOOK
MY PERSONAL BOOK
MY PRIVATE BOOK
MY SECRET BOOK
MY WISH BOOK
CONVERSATION KICKERS

SECOND PRINTING – JANUARY, 1981

Published by Price/Stern/Sloan Publishers, Inc.
410 North La Cienega Boulevard, Los Angeles, California 90048

ISBN:0-8431-0270-5

SPECIAL ME!

The most special thing about me is the way I ____________
____ and
____.

I have a special ____
and a special ____.
Sometimes when I am wearing my ____________________,
I look like a ____.

My ________________________ doesn't think I'm special at all. He (she) thinks I'm just like all the other ____________ ________________ in this world. I would like to set him (her) straight. This is what I would like to say: " ______________
____
____."

The most special thing that I own is my ______________
____.

The most special person that I know is ________________
____.

My most special memory is ______________________
____.

Here are some more things that are very special:

1. ____.
2. ____.

A DAY IN THE LIFE OF ______________________
(your name)

You've probably been wondering what my days are like. Well, I'm going to tell you.

Every morning I get up at ____________. The first thing
(time)
I do is ____, and after that I ____.

When I eat breakfast, I usually have ________________ and ____________________________.

I leave for school at ______________. My teacher's name is ____ and he (she) is very ____________________________. This is what we do every morning: 1. ________________________________;
2. ____;
3. ____.

At lunch I sit with ____________________________ and eat ________________________________ and ________________________________.

After school I usually ____________________________ or ____.

The best thing about my life is ____________________ ____.

The worst thing about my life is ____________________ ____.

LET'S HAVE A CONTEST

I'd like to have a contest with ____________________ and ____________________. This contest would prove who was the best at all kinds of things.

1. We would see who could throw a ball the farthest. I think ____ would win this.
2. We would see who could talk the most. I think ______________________________ would win this.
3. We would see who is the strongest. I think ____________________________ would win this.
4. We would see who is the smartest. I think ______________________________ would win this.
5. We would see who is the nicest. I think ____________________________ would win this.
6. We would see who is the fastest. I think ____________________________ would win this.
7. We would see who is the best-looking. I think ____________________________ would win this.
8. We would see who is the best at sports. I think ____________________________ would win this.

TEN WISHES

1. I wish I owned a great big ______________________________

____.

2. I wish that everybody liked me as much as they like ______

____.

3. I wish that somebody would give me lots of __________

____.

4. I wish I'd find a key to ______________________________.

____.

5. I wish that everybody in my family was ______________

____.

6. I wish that ______________________________________

____________________________________ would be nicer to me.

7. I wish I didn't have to ______________________________

____.

8. I wish I'd never have to see ______________________

____ again.

9. I wish that I could ______________________________

as well as ____.

10. But the thing that I wish the most is ______________

____

____.

BOY, AM I ANGRY!!!!

There are lots of things that make me angry, but __________ __________________________ makes me the angriest of all. I hate it when ______________________________________.
When this happens, I feel like ____________________ ____________________________________.

Here are some other things that make me angry:

1. ____________________________________;
2. ____________________________________;
3. ____________________________________.

When I am angry, I like people to know it. I know people who slam the door really hard when they are angry just so people will know how they feel. Sometimes I do that too, but I also ____________________________________ and ____________________________________.

The worst thing I ever did when I was angry was __________ ____________________________________.
I was kind of sorry about it later, but ______________ ____________________________________.

The best thing to do when you're angry is __________ ____________________________________ ____________________________________.

I'll bet you'd feel a lot better after you'd done that.

A VERY SPECIAL GAME

I'm going to invent a game that is very special. It will be called THE VERY SPECIAL GAME. This game will have lots of special things about it, but the most special thing will be the way it makes me feel.

Whenever I ask this game a question, it will say "You are a very smart ____!"

Whenever I tell this game a joke, it will pat me on the ____ and say, "____

____."

Whenever I write a sentence, this game will read it and say, "You are ____

____!"

This game will have lots of buttons. If you push the red button, the game will spin around and ____________________

____.

If you push the purple button, the game will hug you around the neck and say "____

____."

And if you push the gold button, the game will open its mouth and out will come ____

____________________________. Then it will shut itself off and

____.

WOULDN'T IT BE WILD IF . . .

Wouldn't it be wild if ______________________________ dressed up like a ______________________________ and ______________________________?

Wouldn't it be wild if my ______________________________ bought five ______________________________ and put them in his (her) ______________________________?

Wouldn't it be wild if everybody ate ______________________________ for breakfast and ______________________________ for lunch?

Wouldn't it be wild if my teacher came to school on a ______________________________ and passed out ______________________________ to all the kids?

Wouldn't it be wild if my family lived in a ______________________________ and spent all their time ______________________________?

Wouldn't it be wild if I was allowed to ______________________________ instead of ______________________________?

Wouldn't it be wild if somebody gave me a ______________________________ for my birthday, and ______________________________?

Wouldn't it be wild if my friend ______________________________ came over and we spent the whole day ______________________________?

WHO SAYS I HAVE TO???

Who says I have to eat all my ____________________,
even when I'm not hungry?

My ____________________________ says so, that's who!

Who says I have to go to bed at ____________________
o'clock, even when I'm wide awake?

My ____________________________ says so, that's who!

Who says I have to do homework, even though I know it all?

My ____________________________ says so, that's who!

Who says I have to clean up my room, and __________
____________________, even though it looks just fine to me?

My ____________________________ says so, that's who!

Who says I can't go to ____________________________
until my __________________________________ is finished,
even though we all know that's stupid?

My ____________________________ says so, that's who!

Who say's I'm always wrong, and everybody else is always right?

My ____________________________ says so, that's who!

And why do they say it? Because they're my __________,
and my ____________________________________, and my
____, that's why!!!

A SPECIAL ADVENTURE

I'm planning a very special adventure. I'm planning on filling my suitcase full of ____________________ and flying off to ____________________. Once I get there, I'm planning to change into my ____________ outfit. Then I'm planning to swallow my magic potion. This potion will make me ____________________ so that I'll be able to ____________________.

As soon as I'm ____________________, I'm going to ____________________ and ____________________. People will probably chase me and ____________________, but that will be O.K. because I'll be ____________________.

When my potion wears off, I'll take another potion. This one will make me ____________________ and ____________________, and I'll be able to ____________________ whenever I want to.

If someone tries to steal my potions, I'll just ____________________, and then, when they start to ____________________, I'll tell them to ____________________.

When my adventure is over, I'm sure I'll be ready for a rest. So I'll just hang a sign on my bedroom door that says "____________________." Then I'll climb into bed, pull the covers over my head, and sigh loudly.

SPECIAL PEOPLE

HERE ARE SOME SPECIAL PEOPLE:

________________________ is a special person because ____.

And ____________________ is special too, because he (she) ____________________________________.

________________________ is special because he (she) makes me laugh.

________________________ is special because he (she) makes me feel good about myself.

________________________ is special because of the way he (she) ____________________________.

________________________ is special because he (she) makes me feel like ____________________________.

________________________ is special because he (she) gives me lots of ____________________________.

________________________ is special because he (she) doesn't make fun of me or ____________________ ____.

But ____________________ is the most special person of all, and here are some of the reasons why:

1. ____________________________________;
2. ____________________________________;
3. ____________________________________.

ALL THROUGH THE YEAR

My favorite time of year is ______________________.
I like this time of year because ______________________
____.

The problem with winter is ______________________
______________________ and ______________________.
But I like the winter because ______________________
____ and
____.

Spring is nice because ______________________.
In the spring I can ______________________
and ______________________________________.

Summer is good and bad. It is good because __________
______________________________________. And it is
bad because ______________________________.
In the summer I like to ______________________
____
and ______________________________________.

School starts in the fall, which is ______________
____.
There are other ______________________________
things about the fall, like ______________________
and ______________________________________.

My favorite month of the year is ______________
because ______________________________________.

I LIKE . . .

I like my friend ______________________________________.

I like the way my family ______________________________

____.

I like to lie in bed and listen to ____________________.

I like to visit _______________________________________.

I like stores that sell _______________________________

____.

I like to stay inside and _____________________________

_________________________________ when it is raining.

I like to play with my ________________________________.

I like to read books about ____________________________

____.

I like T.V. shows about _______________________________

____.

I like people who _____________________________________.

On my birthday I like to ______________________________

____.

When I am sad I like to _______________________________

____.

When I am alone I like to _____________________________

____.

I like to eat ____

____.

I DON'T LIKE . . .

I don't like to visit ______________________________.

I don't like the way my family ______________________

____.

I don't like to read books about ____________________

____.

I don't like T.V. shows about ______________________

____.

I don't like people who ___________________________

I don't like to eat _______________________________

____.

I don't like adults who __________________________.

I don't like kids who ____________________________.

I don't like animals who __________________________.

I don't like to play ______________________________

____.

I don't like to go to ______________________________

____.

Here are some other things that I don't like:

1. ____;
2. ____;
3. ____.

I CAN'T BELIEVE IT!!!

I can't believe some of the things people say. For example, ________________________________said the silliest thing the other day. This is what ______________ said: "____.''

Isn't that silly?

And I can't believe some of the dumb things people do. For example, ________________________________ did something REALLY dumb once. This is what __________ did: ____.

Wasn't that dumb?

Sometimes I can't believe my eyes! Once I saw a person who was ____.

And once I read a book about ____. But the strangest thing I've ever heard of was ____.

I've done some pretty dumb and silly things too. Here are some of them:

1. ____;
2. ____.

I'VE HEARD IT ALL BEFORE

I'm tired of people saying the same old things all the time. For example, why do parents always say "____________ ____________," and "____________ ____________?" Why can't they ever say something like "____________?"

And why do teachers always say "____________ ____________," when they could just as easily say "____________?"

When I'm in trouble, people always say "____________ ____________."

And when I'm crying, everybody thinks they have to tell me to ____________.

Sometimes when I'm really happy I shout, "____________ ____________!!" And then my family tells me to ____________.

I wish kids would stop talking about my ____________ ____________ and my ____________. I always want to crawl into a hole and die when they say "____________."

I am the only person who has something interesting to say, and I've been waiting a long time to say it. Here it is: "____________ ____________."

THE PERFECT BIRTHDAY

My next birthday is going to be perfect. When I wake up my room will be piled high with presents. I will slide out of bed and open the one nearest me. I will untie the ______ ribbon and take the lid off the box. Inside the box will be a ______________________________. When I see it I will smile and say, "______________________________."
Then I will move on to the next present. Here are some of the other things that I will get:

1. ______________________________;
2. ______________________________;
3. ______________________________.

When I am dressed, I will go down to breakfast. The table will be covered with ____________________ and when I see it I will smile and say, "____________________." Then I will sit down and ______________________________.

Of course I will not go to school on my birthday. Instead I will ______________________________ and ______________________________.

And that night I will have the best party ever given anywhere. This is why my party will be better than anyone else's.

1. ______________________________;
2. ______________________________.

BAD STUFF

My parents and I don't agree on what's bad. My teacher and I don't agree on what's bad. As a matter of fact, there are lots of people that don't agree with what I think is bad stuff.

For example, my parents think that it is bad to ________ ____________________________________. I don't. I think that ____ is fun. I guess they just don't remember what it's like to be a kid.

My teacher thinks that it's bad to ____________________ _________________________________. I don't. I think it is fun to ____.

My friends and I usually agree on what is bad. But sometimes we don't, and that is when I have a problem. For example, my friends think it is fun to ____________________________ ______________________________. I guess it's kind of fun, but I also don't like it because ___________________________ ____.

But the biggest problem is this: Sometimes my friends want to do something REALLY bad, and I know that if I do it I will get in trouble. But I want my friends to like me. That is a big problem. Usually when this happens, I _____ ____.

GOOD STUFF

My parents and I don't agree on what's good either. For example, my parents think that ______________________________ ______________________________ is good. I don't. Now I'm SURE they don't remember what it's like to be a kid.

I KNOW my teacher doesn't remember what it's like to be a kid. Here are some of the things she (he) thinks are good:

1. ____;
2. ____;
3. ____.

I know some kids who think that ____________________ ______________________________ is good. Isn't that silly?

My friend ____________________ thinks that it is fun to
(name)

____.

And my friend ____________ thinks that ____________ ______________________________________ is the best thing in the whole wide world.

Here are some more things that my parents think are good:

1. ____;
2. ____;
3. ____.

WHO DID IT?

I'm always getting blamed for everything. It's not fair. I'll bet that when I'm not even home people yell, "WHERE'S ______________________? HE (SHE) DID IT AGAIN!!"
(your name)

Sometimes when ________________ breaks something, I know my family thinks I did it. Even if I'm nowhere around. They don't even have to say anything. I can tell.

And sometimes when I'm fighting with ______________ ______________________, my family thinks I started it, even if I didn't. They never tell ________________________ to be quiet! They just yell at me. It's not fair!

Sometimes when I come home from school my _______ meets me at the door. This is what he (she) says: "Can't you EVER ____ ____!" Lots of times I don't even know what he (she) is talking about.

Here are some other things that I get blamed for:

1. ____;
2. ____;
3. ____.

As I said, it's not fair!!

FIGHTS

I hate fights. I don't just mean the "hit him in the head, kick him in the stomach" type of fight. I also mean the kind where everybody's yelling and screaming and your stomach hurts and you feel like crying. I hate all kinds of fights.

Once I got into a fight with ______________________.
This is how it started (I think): ______________________

____

____. I was
so mad that I wanted to ______________________________

____.

After it ended I ______________________________.

When I was little I used to fight with ______________

______________________. I'm not exactly sure why, but
I think it was because ______________________________

____.

The person in my family that I fight with the most is ________

______________________. This is because he (she) is
so ____.

Most of all I hate it when I hear ____________________

____________________ fight. Sometimes I try not to listen, but I can't shut them out. I'd like to tell them how I feel when they fight, but ______________________________

____

____.

I DON'T GET ANYTHING!!

My ____________________ gets EVERYTHING. He (she)
(member of your family)
is definitely the star in this house. I don't even get to ______________________________.

On his (her) birthday, he (she) gets ____________________ ____________________. I get ____________________.

At Christmas, he (she) gets ____________________ ____________. I get ____________________.

He (she) gets a ____________________ for a surprise. I get ____________________ ____________________.

My ______________ gets the best ______________ ______________________________. He (she) gets the first ____________________.

And he (she) ALWAYS is the ____________________.

This is what everybody says to my ______________:
"______________________________
______________________________."

This is what everybody says to me: " ______________
____
______________________________."

You see. I TOLD you that ____________ gets everything.

THE WORST DAY OF ALL

Here is what I think would be the worst day of all:

In the morning, my ______________________________ would tell me to ____.

At school, my teacher would say, "____."

My best friend ______________________________ wouldn't sit next to me because ______________________________________.

____________________________ would trip me and call me a ____
(name)

____.

Somebody (probably ______________________________) would hand out invitations to everybody but me.

A loud bell would ring and the principal would say, "______ ____ ____."

When I got home from school, my ____________________ would ____.

That night we would have ______________________________ for dinner, and then I would find out that the ______________ ____ is broken.

Sometimes I think I've had a bad day, but that would be the worst.